The Aquarium

by Anne Giulieri

To Nana,

I went with Jill
to the aquarium today.

We looked at one big fish tank.
We looked at little fish tanks, too.

In the big fish tank,
we looked at a big gray shark.

Sharks have big white teeth.
They look very scary.

In one little fish tank,
we looked at crabs.
We looked at turtles, starfish,
and sea urchins, too.

In one little fish tank,
we looked at sea horses.
I liked the sea horses.
They swim up and down.
The head of a sea horse
looks like a horse's head.

Sea horses are not in a tank with crabs.

Crabs like to eat sea horses!

13

I liked the aquarium.

Jill liked the aquarium, too!

Can you go to the aquarium with me one day?

It is fun!

Love, Ben

To Nana,
I went with Jill to the aquarium today.
We looked at one big fish tank.
We looked at little fish tanks, too.
In the big fish tank, we looked at a big gray shark.
Sharks have big white teeth.
They look very scary.

In one little fish tank, we looked at crabs.
We looked at turtles, starfish, and sea urchins, too.
In one little fish tank, we looked at sea horses.
I liked the sea horses.
They swim up and down.
The head of a sea horse looks like a horse's head.

Sea horses are not in a tank with crabs.
Crabs like to eat sea horses!
I liked the aquarium.
Jill liked the aquarium, too!
Can you go to the aquarium with me one day?
It is fun!
Love, Ben